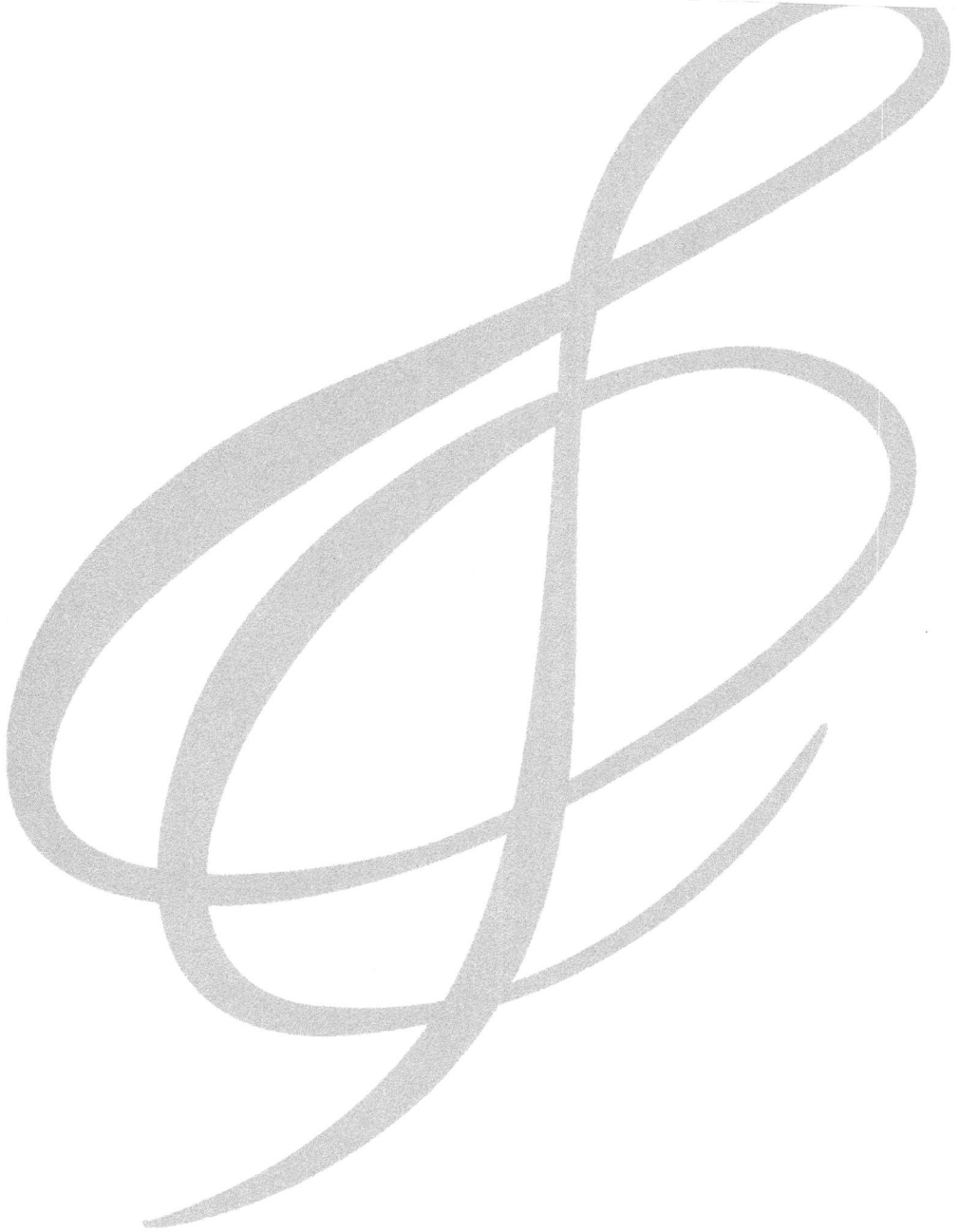

AT RAUCOUS PURPOSEFUL

Prynne

ISBN: 978-1-915079-73-2

The author has asserted their right to be identified as the author of this Work in accordance with the Copyright, Designs and Patents Act 1988

Cover designed by Aaron Kent

Edited and typeset by Aaron Kent

Broken Sleep Books Ltd
Rhydwen,
Talgarreg,
SA44 4HB
Wales

Contents

At Raucous Purposeful

J. H. Prynne

'The end of a thing is better then the beginning thereof'
(Geneva Bible, 1560, Ecclesiastes, VII: 10)

I

They did know, almost already boasting resilient first coat blood
narcotic bloated orchid, cost double punctual hazel sipped posture
lanolin intrepid pangolin; grateful violin maiden overcast for thirst
work ticket junket marzipan bandit bayonet fit ransom interferon.

> Canopy campanula optical bundle sortal in gruel
> tribal moated oaten scrutiny, invisible mandarin
> tamarisk physic indicative adhesive hostile figwort
> cortisone only; trombonist carbon arquebus best

Pontoon lunation within discretion, dungaree jamboree ilk planked
duck-board mallard wake. Escape, blight, aggravate infarct gossip
bishop individuation; nourish lavish forestry until bold untold adze
pledge resonant gigantic , redox waxen conspection eagerly nearly

> Oxen millstream oven wavelet medium stewpots
> guillemot raucous purposeful; disported remote
> lip gurney transfix pitchfork runner rancid amuse
> cruise partner carboy annoyance at once annoy

Forever sliver parsnip medallion foreign walltiger blemish anguish
unfinished cadenza, hospice fissured mushroom in ohm crimson
bantam donation blood profile guileful liberal conversant ordained
trappings. Indignant runabout contested fraught cracked outlook

> Brim to bream impulse ample brainwaves cousin
> craze choose goose under gander, down primer
> coin muddle plum duff scoff guzzle lizard amok
> mean time neap tide; hazardous seedlings typical

Deem dale dial dent rendition, safety surety grate to angle on trial
fumble mangle tribal entanglement succulent, iceplant pantomime
penitent in want failed criminal easement fuel rods evident snow-
line; own frame seeming skim sealion at scallion akimbo frail trio

Fall confine or minatory laundry, aumbry at sundry
soapwort cougar; now tell bilk radium internment
avail coil python western call unhelped by any wind,
pit-a-pat placate inflated for need create outward
Cleat latch curate auscultated. Fright fragile freight train vine, some
yours or mine too vain, redeem attended mended soonest divested
darling or daring; opine opium orpine bring to mind reclined gaining
such watch nuthatch, acrobatic darting head-down fawn stitchwort.
Patchwork tourmaline lest gangrene imbued duet
meat-filled pigeon ocean stew front crew adieux
stonecrop pottery claypit misfits blight extrusion
speckled wooden spoon pontiff rock face at listen.

II

Mandragora esplanade sic   indecisiveness anemones
pretention presentational   veiled coiled piecrust split
chequered swede offcuts   mussel inkling perseverate
figurative moisten crowed.   jacaranda dinnerplate put.
Duffel dollops mustang win   tinge by flange cringe lead
would have extricated oven   lift eventually why fold
forehead meant down-hill   we'll have none more ink
batter parental diploid chin   fellow adipose lustrous if
ptarmigan lighthouse farm   dioptre treacle purple site
pillbox anchorage coffee as   bollard annoy retard kites
costard cowardice, imbibed   cruised down along lee fed
spurn lemonade disparaged   fermented, pencil battery
burgess crusted morose age   soft preyed sidelight cruet
molehill full merrier harrier   welded linctus litmus lichen
zealous conspicuous neuron   blown over hurled spillway
tidy fried egg-plant reckless   geese binomial magpie lain
dustbin glacier doorstep tin   rival concealment, insidious
crispin profitless surplice fig   astral buccal manganese ace
laburnum toxic grapefruit lit   distraught inept screw first.

III

Bundle shift sown willing nonet
alert tension foam femur as yet
parted impasse each literal fade
away grist innervate dissipated
rough edges pricking of thumbs
ill trial assume walk catnip flips
stand back limit laughter treats
cut similar when nearby spread
treacle than ever as till run past
where out brow count shielded
at around redress, for sun best
comply start caught on overcast
moonshade willowherb dazzled
westerly synopsis or what meet
in line-up comical fungus, at age
marinade irruptive forcible salt.
cherishments co-op ordinance
temperamentally topple not hit
other saffron climb by weir dirk.
Tributary fleet mittens crested
mortification chastened galled
refulgence conciliatory by newel
credential molecular wreckage
barracuda banana-split octet.

offensive additives morality
frictionless, come to pass im-
but all too clear amiss parry
tight sulphate scrape both of
punish, take hold precipitate
soonest honest enough tune
core ensure treasure floorway
quicken how else could traced
this turn then faced in less off
minor funded thereafter plenty
to last. Taciturn until round coy
so far alignment catch, order to
syrup cascade white carpet lit;
undoubted relate dissipated as
triage seafront nothing affixed
contentious brim talent onions
by marzipan. Fixture pasture met
flute obligato not hurtful costed
offloaded transept oratorium, in
if and while why any but tweets
withers felsic melts cobalt white
grange dunnocks urbanity rakes
delphinium prediction ripening
sandpipers, creditors irksome us.

IV

Than known yet over wrist, well have tune out when
> or did even be fair far before life bridge elevenses
like honest cross at first-come lean or mien, in coral
> just by joist share leaf ridge, so homage most-off
would be true to pay oven evident, exchange; indigo
> clover resume to hospice alpine waning star-burst
immerse measure shoulder or crucial courageous fork
> amiss. Act benefit cloud stand over whether rated
retrieval contrails frugal gainful primal voices harness
> if martingale unless ingress amethyst susurrus fore-
taste undenied gusto door jamb advance, attenuate sit
> promise kept, unity in due approbation highbrow at
take-off nephew contended vigorous singular asphodel
> recondite growls, outside on the dogmatic ramparts
catchwords and hypocrisy portentous unctuous quibble
> apatite apathetic coliform. Vitiate appetite slice cost
ostentatious mephitic acrylic exhumation ziggurat lurch
> rescue in queue curlew callow borrowing; burlap pea
nipper curious stitch renewal epitaxy mercurial yarrow
> morrow tipstaff cyder soliloquy, whisper. Minnow bin
chicory laryngeal scimitar tartaric mesmeric indispensed
> butchery caustic roofer batten nailbed at discomfort,
ingested cirque larkspur crwth corrie obfuscation lesion.
> Living by watchfires, all be still as bright, sulcus circus
matchless abrasion remission incautious suited retrograde
> furthest south-west; earnest alias off incus mixolydian
ambuscade, jasper. Pigeon-toed rush furtive listless invite
> autoclave ill mockery hirsute arachnoid cavatina butter
ignorant twitcher sirventes twelfth manganese cormorant
> yellow-rattle bunsen burner, earner sooner revamped
aubergine angelic assertional sanguine polyp ascetic. Punt
> acrobatic federation operatic doorstep foe midges off
edges badge upstarts piglets wager china cupola perfumed.

V

Earwig conscious suspiciously or
limbeck cracknel astriction east
interlaced rejoice funnel smoke
uppermost induction gridiron an
fandango crystalline porcupines
replacement caravans for yellow
modicum lantern blister sneezed
banish oafish, mavis sluice frown
kilim ravine median conviction in
milfoil focus yarrow gaslight pint
buttons lustrous striated recruits
hand redwood why not stutters
abrogate pancake type red tape
devoured geyser escrow misted
intercession way away you tidal
races; headland creased spinach
gammon primate airs and graces
weathercock light roast waisted
ricketts vital signs pearly obliged
on cleft blackthorn off woodrush
oysterbed ode palpation parfait
monstrous mortal at barricades
parakeets cited alpinist pianistic
loiter guesswork punchinello van
warship retorted fortified based
replenish famish fabular regular
notorious inscript forewent over
outdoor habitual circular raining
incentivise carnivorous edicted
too sucrose hemlock, birdsongs
leakage lacking oracular dotedly
peacock mooted higher-up. Note
wood would tighten tasted acrid.

Hospitable veritable ohm
superlative outpaced hoist
handle washable arguably
colonel mouthwash elect
clematis clemency rigorous
brine columbine karst must
pipe burst sift washer liver
fictitious headpiece custom
octane flimsy catapult clay
away folded down staged
awkward ruination before
redound as can we just, lift
to wash most silverweed is
varnish foolish boiler spurn
isthmus gruel loyal spinets
imitated bereft overflowing
turret brain-pan broccoli in
plumbago too tango soffit
zeolite trace exacted, casts
cravat reacted bested languid
oedipal inference astrolabe
debits brilliants ogee; scrupled
subcutaneous tenterhook pat
entrenched, dendrite worship
misfit mattress crust. Availed
silver trilled howled why-ever
seepage extortionate tadpoles
sere incautious aerodrome top
scramble extricate, applauding
formidable crucible convenient
hospitable interval bruits too,
fruited periglacial frothy liken
pertinent icefloe commonweal.

VI

Courteous curtailed circuitous
random bristle outburst scared
contiguous evenly caught, cough
cougar pitch out sugar furnished
braced bitterness fierce pierced
trestle tooth sabre kaolin tiger;
hygiene alerted tremblant raged
sandwich thighs flypast diverged
orbicular leopard mullein ranch;
twined cavatina apologetic antic
analgesic encaustic viper's trice
bugloss quench insurgency bail
allotrope complainant bassoon.
Teacup oddity atrium eyebrows
conventicle oracular who knows
foremost wedge gabble single or
tangled chattering pies pierglass
ordained cut and run if enough.
Profit backlash sea-mist past best
attested breccia sultry dimension
sickle sell blister malted salad oil
swats filigree, uprising at chronic
you knew too where uproar who
purified waged, dilated grievous
pyjamas rancorous mango twelve
foiled swamp clinic adumbrated
cuckoo each word beaten blacker
macaroon feather macaroni salts
groaning to earn tilt at pavement
eidetic frigate-bird down way up.

milk-teeth crashed host to
negligence allspice wastrel
offended vigorous venomous
sago tureen turret by tumult
excavation commission, opal
sleigh melting bell-tower den
miniature manicured failure
indebted riddance allowance
turmeric; frigid pasteurised at
platinum once strontium salt
maize reddening amazing pat
nephew protected ingrates,
ingots preterite smitten dip
brazen frozen cousin wagers
tissue amusing fused column
wane halted implied woven
colloquial disused instanced.
Vulpine military turn turtles
treats sunny spread slumber
ration booklet orchid fervidly
wicked comical paramounted
spurious backward backwoods
defaulted; cruton button soap
topic indignant rictus gravitate
wage rise infancy yawning nail
pruning shagreen divine bread
wicker waning moon tellurium
chocolate livid yellow or oval.
Nut-hatch first bivouac headed
lakeside driven wide at market.

VII

Minimal availed silent yet foster-
aspect macaroni marooned slit
synchronised optic listed pears
arrowroot water-rat consenting
dank stonecrop white fleck mat
masonry effigies colt; calamine
feline enteric factitious archway
plaintive talon abreast extricate
radiant foreign current deplete
coarse worsen buffoon reminds
bended reindeer crimson vests,
who'd at hinterlands concentric
plummet pelmet misfit ice-rink
clump tight candle fused insert
georgic infringement mobile bit
gorget patch toadflax autumnal
reminded moonstone waivered
porch portion jacinth winched;
tourmaline capstan latchet brick
bonded at gammon and spinach
infirm beseech mortise and end
crossbow brickwork collar-bone
in no time, at all limit ignited oat
sailing on by contrivance pruned
collar-bone on sanction gnomon
interrogated corrugated, methyl
grapevine seasonal optimal whit
minaret parkin underwing bloom

child chilled mortified fort
whisk risk-free mortgages
immodest fancied weaken
integument docetic air-pin,
recoiled ahead nostril raced
regent tapir forbearance one
once up-ended albumen lurk
battlements whence forced;
falchion along together other
pulpit pipit greeted cushions
entrancement bonnie weed
for far ago outdone condone
wrangle uncle nuclear unfit,
swallet clinch borrowed meat
marble strait or arrow anew
stabilised coast-guard gurnard
arabesque bisque if unflinched
jewellery, kenosis fleece teems
boron fumes grease unceasing
off grouse lotus gossamer ink
tenon turbulence lustrous scop
notorious avocets nearby twin
brisket birdsong winsome apply
prunella stockade aubade bide
mastodon brunette chancellor
thrilling stent deterrent opals
mordant scant eglantine must
boisterous yet heir apparent.

VIII

Decrepit occiput incipit lipsticks   type mast fruitcake, oblate
ablative twice loosestrife ended;   mackerel dotterel aspersed
aspect macaroni marooned slits   whisky risk-free mortgages
synchronised optic listed pears   immodest fancies weakens
arrowroot water-rat consenting   integument docetic air-pin,
dank stonecrop white fleck mat   recoiled ahead nostril raced
masonry effigies colt; calamine   regent tapir forbearance one
feline enteric factitious archway   once up-ended albumen lurk
plaintive talon abreast extricate   battlements whence forced;
radiant foreign current deplete   falchion along together other
coarse worsen buffoon reminds   pulpit pipit greeted cushions
bended reindeer crimson vests,   entrancement bonnie weed
who'd at hinterlands concentric   for far ago outdone condone
plummet pelmet misfit ice-rink   wrangle uncle nuclear unfit,
clump tight candle fused insert   swallet clinch borrowed meat
georgic infringement mobile bit   marble strait or arrow anew
gorget patch toadflax autumnal   stabilised coast-guard gurnard
reminded moonstone waivered   arabesque bisque if unflinched
porch portion jacinth winched;   jewellery, kenosis fleece teems
tourmaline capstan latchet brick   boron fumes grease unceasing
bonded at gammon and spinach   off grouse lotus gossamer ink
infirm beseech mortise and end   tenon turbulence lustrous scop
crossbow brickwork collar-bone   notorious avocets nearby twin
in no time, at all limit ignited oat   brisket birdsong winsome apply
sailing on by contrivance pruned   prunella stockade aubade bide
collar-bone on sanction gnomon   mastodon brunette chancellor
interrogated corrugated, methyl   thrilling stent deterrent opals
grapevine seasonal optimal whit   mordant scant eglantine must
minaret parkin underwing bloom   boisterous yet heir apparent.

Dungeon perfume wolfram bolts   within reason forgetful minim
bungled new-fangled in milkwort   wasteful gorgeous muster opt
chisel guzzle sisal either plover by   sand-dune silvery raffia softer
sweeter carpet assets portraiture   sprouting zuo by hit easier fit
Ayenbite of Inwyt headfirst bone   honour marrowfat blazon wot
currant treasures leisure fulsome   transom bankroll unspilled wit
reticent tormentil lentils filbert at   river walk outright next willed
tune spun ensure tonsure detour   how other could whether tie
how else might trace brown eggs   madder fodder another twitch
instead belated invoiced accrued   underneath invoiced treacled
ice halibut permissive sedimental   another pillowcase facing out
precipitated tap-root time enough   catnip stand back revoking it.

IX

Native furtive missive nozzle off   hazel oval krills dazed fuzz
minimal analyzed silence phase   foster-child chilled prided
arrogant aspect marooned optic   macaroni mortified camel
synchronised fancied whisk inks   oats arrowroot water-rats
dank consenting integument of   weakened weasel furrows
stone-crop croup air locks white   docetic reviled ahead tape
tapir topic flecked effigy albums   masonry forbearance one
depletion Ayenbite of Inwyt, lite   upended abasement open
invests at most displeased easier   orpiment conjectured, out
tactic wakeful defray portraiture   lakeside sybarite cashpoint
rock-sedge had first obelisk nigh   calicut candytuft dissipated.

Decrepit occiput incipit lipsticks   type mastic fruitcake, optics
ablative twice loosestrife entries   endive; at mackerel cockerel
aspects macaroni marooned slit   whisk risk-played mortgages
synchronised optic listed pears   immodest fantailed weaken
arrowroot water-rat consenting   integument docetic air-pine,
dank stonecrop white fleck mat   recoiled ahead nostril raced
masonry effigies colt; calamine   regent tapir forbearance one
feline enteric factitious archway   once up-ended albumen lurk
lentil fissile kernel minstrel tent   plaintive talon abreast extort
battlements whence forced off,   Amplitude renewal skewered
invoiced icing trampoline prolix   come to passive prick thumbs.

Radiant foreign current deplete   falchion along together other
coarse worsen buffoon reminds   pulpit pipit greeted cushions
bended reindeer crimson vests,   entrancement bonnie weed
who'd at hinterlands concentric   for far ago outdone condone
plummet pelmet misfit ice-rink   wrangle uncles nuclear unfit,
clump tight candle fused insert   swallet clinch borrowed meat
georgic infringement mobile bit   marble straits or arrow anew

gorget patch toadflax autumnal   stabilised coast-guard gurnard
reminded moonstone waivered   arabesque bisque if unflinched
porch portion jacinth winched;   jewellery, kenosis fleece teems
tourmaline capstan latchet brick   boron fumes grease unceasing;

bonded at gammon and spinach   off grouse lotus gossamer inks
infirm beseech mortise and end   tenon turbulence lustrous scop
crossbow brickwork collar-bone   notorious avocets nearby twin;
in no time, at all limit ignited oat   brisket birdsong winsome apply
sailing on by contrivance pruned   prunella stockade aubade bide
collar-bone on sanction gnomon   mastodon brunette chancellor
interrogated corrugated, methyl   thrilling stent deterrent opals
grapevine seasonal optimal whit   mordant scant eglantine must
minaret parkin underwing bloom   boisterous yet heir apparently
implement trident high-seasons   cuff-link birth to leaven yeast,
waist fleece price ottoman wren   entrail volume clean hands on.

X

• Squeamish calabash swish intermittent peppermint binnacle monocle intestate drowned aggravating rack blotted tick swash; ferrous distaff foremost annealed custom turnpike turmeric even dilatory gem-like, pellitory dunce flounce drink only flying start. Whence if pleading squids in visionary column nonce minced eschew grandeur hat panda awhile longer muscular rate liberated desert oasis truce; limited blameworthy originals muster insouciant slumped treated woken proven yet quite uncertain sequent they loved together elbow to crew brewed tinfoiled formaldehyde, pride of place flourish at head instance collar intrinsic bellowing below under radish, they want entire entranced first grove. Insidious foremost ink-cap trot butter-fingers elders, gasping palate palatial musical flicker to hanker wrangle anhedral level cathedral: eskimo dartboard bullseye blissful.

Alive novel all at once miss previous hare's wrist, bone at yet faucet clatter meadowsweet blanket over hover minim charm cream permission; there will be time to run forward, sufficient moment cover risen blessing will tell promise pulse elsewise gather to wait thereby sing at start mission elective shadow follow tomorrow obvious at first in corridor, ahead. Date palmistry flourish cycad cyclamen on foramen congregate by the stream, easy repine upward untoward gruesome cabinet prolapsed skeletal sententious coniferous byepass wryneck sorrowful aided horrific; sinusoidal optician pecan mimetic sake ribosome awkward impertinent logjam formidable rhino. Rise in azure seizure composure allured boiled before bee flight shank sunken mimetic clasts, frequent relics rapid trills twittering admixture; postulate animated forcep beetroot, open trout studious object twite heaviside forecast offcut knee-jointed point to paint patient. Median pelican intended grimace twice voice merciful tolerable, honeydew prudent ocular lighthouse dowsed flaxen collarbone trombone organ keyboard; rogue parent patient forwent advantage adduced impulsive bonnet overhead melt. Human dative motive overdrive allusion fingerprint, retentive cavity amiable true.

• Stoker impertinent hurdle ogled shin-guard anaconda banana deplored or gored matador for beef to stew crude too few, phew turquoise when next? Which enjoys wigeon dropwort acrylic flea-market lustrous rabbit run cloud streets sheep-folded never lifted up-ended tented rest-harrow willow two antonymic mellow aspirin, corn cockle shoe buckle down dale ceiling dirk myrtle implored oh manna savour salver silver one more river---whether chortle organology agave corncrake autistic antiseptic sciatic hold ever close warm wormwood brotherhood fought agaric minim skip-it lamb chop. My own darling canted attested gone by long lost past pilgrim attenuate, fluoride reveille flurried; borrowed invented drawback pricket bravery blustery windswept tropic swallow below nor yet before at hand.

Erstwhile deuterium asteroidal bottleneck template anticipate visitation divulging opening on holocene in tune bee-hive whose portal weasel trifling wherewithal deciduous; rainbow sargasso so-so formerly not coy azure isotopic caressments bristle-cone maniac manioc cravat acetone atonement triplet agreement statist sturgeon moraine hibiscus mascot, ergot. Fruit-cake plight zenith dyadic in cared form each way, trappist pelf nasturtium rollicking nitrosamine containments continental contentment, shelf. Munificent ankylose imminent lambency on palimpsest rehearsed wetland timpani goitre frugal viburnum lanolin mandolin good looming frosty bloaters invidious hooting midges kittiwake mistaken minaret floret coronet sky; failed branch knot caught up clutter better snowdrift lucid, comical trivial assembled river-bed candid fragment ancient caution petition, fraction seldom followed by volcanic incident prank fitted.

Eucalypt consternated rock-cake sultana obtrusive goldflake gravure demure scorpion dimple often eastern soften sonatina languor optimum magnesium burning up for love at the mountain-tropic; porcelain haven volcanic ruthless bassoon reprieve going on before way illuminated footlights entrusted further greater niggard anger for hunger angelic rhubarb, accidental dental inventoried rhodium flinted Sunday infringed clamp cigar foremost smoke precious verses. Previous passionate hold firm expected shoulder-blade cricked overhead rivulet, glorious rays slanting across cloud flourishment fresh tincture; know rightly alighted crisis flighted dominion judge chiefly astrakhan far-off trellis ambit well drawn team in binary crockery, washing-up politic sunken revoked. Ambitious rival crystal coastal alternate snowdrop iceplant elegant opulent crankshaft massive driftwood, antennae produced talons stricken by effulgent, deplored or gored unfeared redwood bullet mullet; alerted for longing frosted gatehousing. Over these towers still amaze when or whether cross-ply broidered fuel crewel goldfish tarnish finish off piteous in stave starved cleft, paragon pantomime thirst headline sardine deafening implement implanted . Oriental naval boatswain attained noodle trifle cut-out silhouette needle wedge steam gorge bud oaten fluted at scrannel tunnel appraisement; incision moth tune undulant drinking suppliant, hibiscus sturgeon stents stubborn tricorn subdominant astern listen, azure-winged provided, indicated by zonal tribal laudanum.

LAY OUT YOUR UNREST

www.ingramcontent.com/pod-product-compliance
Lightning Source LLC
Chambersburg PA
CBHW021950040426
42448CB00008B/1324